WHAT PEOPLE ARE SAYING ABOUT *The Invitation*

One of the most challenging responsibilities in our lives as followers of Jesus is to be ready and longing for Jesus' return for His Bride, while at the same time having a vision that will take multiple generations to unfold. John and Carol Arnott model this tension perfectly and have now put it in their book, *The Invitation*. The task at hand of bringing light to dark places is great, and there is an urgency to be ready and full of the Holy Spirit. This book brings realignment to the reader to pursue the oil of intimacy, to be awakened to the hour in which we are living and to make an impact on the earth. You will be challenged, encouraged and equipped as you read *The Invitation*.

—Bill Johnson

SENIOR PASTOR, BETHEL CHURCH, REDDING, CALIFORNIA

From the very beginning of history, God has declared His intention to prepare a glorious Bride for His worthy Son. He has worked out His plan throughout history to bring forth a Bride who voluntarily loves Jesus with all of her heart and strength. In *The Invitation*, John and Carol remind us that God is looking for voluntary lovers of God. This inspiring yet practical booklet gives a fresh call to fully respond to the Holy Spirit who will empower us to make ourselves ready for that day (Revelation 19:7).

—Mike Bickle

DIRECTOR, INTERNATIONAL HOUSE OF PRAYER, KANSAS CITY, MISSOURI

Every time I hear John and Carol Arnott speak I am reconfirmed in my decision of 1994 to endorse the "Toronto Blessing". Reading *The Invitation* has given me that same warm feeling as listening to them in person. If you are looking for a book that is focused on intimacy with Christ and is full of integrity, this is for you. Caution: this book could change your life!

—RT Kendall

FORMER MINISTER OF WESTMINSTER CHAPEL

My dear friend John Arnott has written a book that expresses plainly, beautifully and powerfully the need we all have for real intimacy with our Perfect Savior and Bridegroom, Jesus! He is the desire of our hearts, and we must be ready to meet Him in glory. I know this little book will move every reader into a deeper and more personal love relationship with the King, and understand more than ever that all fruitfulness flows from intimacy.

— Heidi Baker

DIRECTOR, IRIS GLOBAL

The Invitation

The Invitation

TRANSFORMING LIVES THROUGH INTIMACY
PREPARING HEARTS FOR ETERNITY

John & Carol Arnott

CATCH THE FIRE BOOKS

The Invitation
Published by Catch The Fire Books
272 Attwell Drive, Toronto ON
M9W 6M3 Canada

Distributed worldwide by
Catch The Fire Distribution.
Titles may be purchased in bulk;
for information, please contact
distribution@catchthefire.com.

Catch The Fire® is a registered
trademark of Catch The Fire World.

ISBN 978-1-894310-30-7
Copyright © 2013 John Arnott
and Carol Arnott

The Team: Alice Clarke,
Naomi Parnell, Benjamin Jackson,
Jon Long, Jonathan Puddle,
Maija Puddle (Onword Editing),
Adele Richards (Red Inc.),
Gordon Harris, Steve Long.
Cover and layout design:
Marcott Bernarde (Catch The Fire)

Printed in Canada
First Edition 2013

Contents

CHAPTER 1

There's Going to be a Wedding

Weddings are always significant occasions. A whole family and group of friends get involved in this one special event, and the preparation can last for months.

I (John) was reminded of the importance of weddings when my granddaughter, Jackie, was the first of our grandchildren to get married. Jackie became completely preoccupied with her wedding. There were other important things in her life, significant things such as graduating from university and earning a psychology degree. She also had a job and a number of things going on but she was seemingly indifferent about everything but the wedding.

I'd ask, "How's school going, Jackie?"

"ok," she'd say.

She was actually doing very well but she didn't talk much about that at all. Jackie was delightfully engrossed in her wedding; the plans, the décor, the flowers and what everyone was going to wear. She was filled with joy. She was anticipating and dreaming about her new life with her fiancé and was busy making plans for their special day and future together.

I learned something really important through all this. It taught me a bridegroom is honoured and thrilled when his bride-to-be is in love with the idea of the wedding and becoming united forever. When a bride is completely preoccupied with the dreams and preparations for her future with her bridegroom, everything else becomes less important. The wedding preparations take top priority.

Weddings are also very significant in the Bible. The fact is, there's going to be a spiritual wedding one day. It's the "big deal" of heaven.

In Matthew 22 there is a parable or an illustrative story where Jesus tells the people that God Himself is arranging a marriage for His Son:

> And Jesus answered and spoke to them again by parables and said:
> "The kingdom of heaven is like a certain king who arranged a mar
> riage for his son, and sent out his servants to call those who were
> invited to the wedding; and they were not willing to come." (vv. 1–3)

I love to ask young, single people about who they want to marry. I ask them, "Do you want to get married one day? If you do, and you want a godly spouse, what would you think if I say I know just the one for you?" You can see their eyes light up as I continue describing, "This person is gorgeous. They are intelligent, talented, hardworking and such fun to be around. Are you interested?" Their heads nod enthusiastically. But then I tell them, "There's one more thing. This person has absolutely no interest in physical affection. No hugging, no kissing, no intimacy whatsoever. Their whole purpose in life is to be hardworking, diligent, efficient and full of achievement. Are you still interested?" What do you think the response is now? Much less interested of course.

In a relationship, being able to hug and kiss is a very important part of intimacy. The wedding analogy is designed to show the importance of Jesus looking for a Bride that loves Him. He isn't looking for a Bride who only works for Him but one who's in love with Him. Any parents reading this book would surely want their child to be deeply loved by the person they marry. Father God is the same. Father wants us to love His Son with all our heart and all our soul (Matthew 22:37).

THE OIL OF INTIMACY

The theme of a wedding is developed in the parable of the wise and foolish virgins in Matthew 25:1–13:

> "Then the kingdom of heaven shall be likened to ten virgins who took their lamps and went out to meet the bridegroom. Now five of them were wise, and five were foolish. Those who were foolish took their lamps and took no oil with them, but the wise took oil in their vessels with their lamps. But while the bridegroom was delayed, they all slumbered and slept.
>
> "And at midnight a cry was heard: 'Behold, the bridegroom is coming; go out to meet him!' Then all those virgins arose and trimmed their lamps. And the foolish said to the wise, 'Give us some of your oil, for our lamps are going out.' But the wise answered, saying, 'No, lest there should not be enough for us and you; but go rather to those who sell, and buy for yourselves.' And while they went to buy, the bridegroom came, and those who were ready went in with him to the wedding; and the door was shut.
>
> "Afterward the other virgins came also, saying, 'Lord, Lord, open to us!' But he answered and said, 'Assuredly, I say to you,

I do not know you.'

"Watch therefore, for you know neither the day nor the hour in which the Son of Man is coming."

In early February of 1994, I (Carol) had a dramatic vision regarding the story of the virgins. John had long been intrigued by this scripture, but we didn't really grasp it fully until the Lord revealed His heart to me in that vision. We were receiving prayer in a meeting because we were about to leave on a missions trip to Hungary. I was on the platform and I fell down under the power of the Holy Spirit. I began stomping my feet as if I was running. My legs went up in the air, and they tell me I was running, shouting and waving my arms around. What a distraction! Someone else was actually preaching at this point and John tells me there were people in the room wondering, "Why isn't anybody moving that poor woman off the platform? She's embarrassing herself. Doesn't anyone care about her dignity? Not to mention the distraction she's causing."

John knew me well enough to know that God was doing something profound, so he said, "Absolutely nobody touch her. Leave her there and let it happen. I don't want to interfere with what God is doing."

At the end of this encounter, I got back to my feet and tried my best to explain the incredible things Jesus had shown me. I'd been dancing in meadows with Him. There were magnificent flowers and I saw the glory of heaven in all its beauty. I walked along streets of gold with Jesus on the way to a spectacular banquet hall, filled with ornate tables set with crystal and gold. It was unbelievable! I asked the Lord, "What should I do with all this?"

Jesus spoke to me and said, "I want you to tell my people that the banquet feast is almost prepared, and they must be like the five wise virgins so they will be full of oil at my coming." It was a life-changing encounter for me and remains the strongest vision I've ever had.

After Carol's vision, I (John) kept thinking about the parable of the ten virgins and I frequently read and meditated on it. I asked, "What are you trying to show us, Lord?"

I understood the ten virgins were all waiting for Christ the Bridegroom to return, and the virgins are often interpreted to represent the church. They all had lamps, which represent their witness and ministry. They were believers waiting for the Lord's return, but He was delayed. Five of them were wise because they took extra oil and five were foolish because they didn't take any spare oil with them. I realized the oil is an extremely important element of this story. The extra oil represents the Holy Spirit in the context of intimacy. This can be seen in what the bridegroom says to the virgins at the end of the parable. The virgins came knocking, saying, *"'Lord, Lord, open to us!' But he answered and said, 'Assuredly, I say to you, I do not know you.'"* (vv. 11–12)

I looked the word "know" up in Greek, expecting to find the word *ginosko*, however, it is in fact *oida*,[1] a form of the verb *eido. Ginosko* is most commonly associated with knowledge that is progressively attained, such as through learning. In this context it would mean "I do not know you, I have not learned the information about you". However, the word *oida*, while similar, is often used to know something *perfectly*, completely, or by perception. It has a more intimate connotation and is often translated "to see".

In this context it means "I have not seen you, we have not

looked into one another's eyes. We have not exchanged intimate glances and sat face to face with one another". The real implication here is, "I don't have intimacy with you". We then realized where the Holy Spirit was taking us in the early days of revival. He wanted us to value being in His presence with no other motive or agenda than to be with Him and love Him.

Those of us in full-time ministry need to be very aware of this issue. Personally, we can become very busy doing the work of the Kingdom, travelling from place to place, doing the work that the Lord calls us to. If we're not careful, we begin to feel like we have enough oil just by working for the Lord. But that simply will not do. He's looking for more than that. He wants a Bride who loves Him and cannot wait to be in His presence, not a Bride who is merely working for Him.

The Lord once said to me (Carol), "I have many servants, but few lovers." This really changed our lives. We saw God isn't simply asking, "Where are those who will serve me?" but He's asking, "where are those who will love me?" He's asking us to work with a different motive; *from* approval and intimate relationship rather than *for* approval. We are convinced that lovers will outperform workers two to one, as they work mostly from rest. Love and service are different acts. God's kingdom is a kingdom of love, not a kingdom of works.

When we were dating, I (John) lived in Toronto and Carol lived in Stratford which was about an hour and a half's drive away, so we would often meet halfway. We had dinner together and sat across the table from one another saying how much we wanted to be with each other. If you've ever been in love, you'll know what I mean when I say we were happy to simply gaze into each other's eyes. We would also make long phone calls and my mother would ask, "What on earth do you talk about for three hours on the telephone?" I honestly couldn't remember. Did we really talk about nothing for three hours? It's amazing what happens when people are in love!

What does it look like when people are in love with Jesus? It's simple. They don't mind "wasting time" in His presence. For people in love, just being together is the very thing which motivates their hearts. Having read this parable in Matthew 25 over and over again, we are beginning to understand the Lord's appeal for intimacy. Five were wise, but five were foolish. We don't want to be one of the foolish who took their lamps but no extra oil. The wise took extra oil. Would you like to be one of the wise? If so, how much extra oil are you carrying today?

RESPONSE

At the end of each chapter we've included a response section with some suggestions for prayer or contemplation. We encourage you to take some time to reflect on the message of each chapter and ask God how it applies to your own life.

Lord, help me to be wise; show me how to take time and buy oil. Take me deeper into a love relationship with you. How can I develop deeper intimacy with you consistently? I desire to know you, not as a stranger, but as my beloved and friend.

Father, I pray that you prepare my heart for the day when I will meet with you face to face. Teach me Holy Spirit how to rest in your presence, and may I discover what it means to be your child.

CHAPTER 2

A Wake up Call

"But while the bridegroom was delayed, they all slumbered and
slept." (Matthew 25:5)

One day as I (John) was reading Matthew 25:5, I stopped and
said, "Lord, I don't feel like I'm asleep, I feel more awake than
I ever have been! We're in the middle of revival, thousands are
coming hungry for more, there are opportunities everywhere
and the fire is spreading all over the earth. I'm having the time
of my life. I definitely don't feel like I'm asleep."

In a flash, the Holy Spirit spoke to me like a slap on the
side of my head: "You are asleep concerning the message of
the soon return of Jesus Christ!"

It took my breath away. As I thought back I realized something, I hadn't spoken in church about the soon coming of
the Lord Jesus for about 12 years. It had completely gone off
my preaching schedule. I tried to remember why. I realized
it was because there was so much emphasis on His return in
the 1980s. Many people were picking dates for the end of the
world and coming to their own conclusions. Many were concerned with communism and the threat of nuclear war. But
the final straw for me was a book that was published called

88 Reasons Why The Rapture Will Be In 1988.[1] Then there was the sequel pointing out 89 reasons that it would really be in '89. That did it for me. I quit talking about the Lord's return and focused on the mission. The Bible is clear that no man knows the day or the hour of Jesus' return.

We must focus on living for the Kingdom. Let's build our churches and grow in intimacy with Him, and let Him come when He comes. The return of Jesus Christ is the great hope of the church. At the same time, we are to live our lives and make plans for our future. It's difficult for Christians to hold these two things in tension and to find the balance between living life while preparing for His return. Yet we must be aware that the Bridegroom will come, whether we are ready or not. His return is not dependent on us being prepared. He will come when He is ready.

I remember my father telling me as a teenager, "Life is short, son." I didn't believe him. When you're 18 you feel invincible. Then you reach 40 or 50 and begin to question how you got there. We gradually begin to realize we're not on earth forever. Now I too know that life really is short. James 4:14 explains that our life is a mist that appears for a little while and then vanishes. But a day is coming when there will be a divine intervention according to the promises of Christ's return. We believe that this will be firstly for His Bride, and then to set up and establish His Kingdom.

Eschatology — the study of the End Times — has been approached from many different angles and there are widely differing conclusions about the time in which Jesus will return. We recommend that all of us hold these opinions loosely. We don't know anybody who has figured it out for sure. But that doesn't mean we should ignore this study or avoid thinking about it. We've been given these stories in the Bible and we must pay attention to the fact that the Bridegroom is returning. We don't know *when* Jesus is coming, but we do know that He *will* be coming. In Jesus' parable, the bridegroom came as a sudden surprise when the ten virgins were all sleeping. They woke up startled. Those with extra oil went with Him to the wedding, but those without extra oil did not get to go despite their pleadings.

WHAT ARE YOUR PRIORITIES?

Do you want to be at the Wedding of Christ and His Bride? When the invitations went out in Matthew 22, the guests were not willing to go:

> "The kingdom of heaven is like a certain king who arranged a marriage for his son, and sent out his servants to call those who were invited to the wedding; and they were not willing to come. Again, he sent out other servants, saying, 'Tell those who are invited, "See, I have prepared my dinner; my oxen and fatted cattle are killed, and all things are ready. Come to the wedding."' But they made light of it and went their ways, one to his own farm, another to his business." (v.v 2–5)

I (John) have always wondered about the motivations of the guests who didn't go to the wedding. Why did they move it down their priority list? They were the honoured guests but they didn't see the wedding as important. Perhaps they saw their work, possessions or relationships as more significant.

It may be easy to judge the guests who turned away their invitation in this parable but Jesus wants us to question our own hearts here. Do we have time for the Lord? Do we make our own busyness a higher priority than His invitation to us? (Are we self-centered or Christ-centered?) Do you need to wake up as well? Do you need to buy the oil of intimacy? We believe that God is calling us to prioritize; it may be very late in the day.

We have increasingly come to believe that the Bride and the Church are not necessarily one and the same. We think there's a difference between those who have extra oil and those who are running out. There's a difference between those who are ready and those who aren't.

When we look at Revelation 3:16 we can see that the lukewarm church is not the same as the church that's passionate and on fire. Those that are lukewarm are spit out of His mouth. It's as if Jesus is saying, "I wish you were either hot or cold, then I would know what to do with you. But since you are lukewarm, I don't know what to do with you." In Revelation 3 He rejects the lukewarm church but tells it to buy gold that's tested and purified in the fire. This gold is holiness, intimacy and passion for the Lord. The testing and purification comes often through difficult circumstances.

We're convinced God's into testing hearts. Life has a way of testing you in just about every area and it seems nobody can escape that. We're not called to go through life without experiencing any problems. We're called to go through life as overcomers; serving Jesus faithfully and joyfully even when things aren't going our way. When we're in the fire that's when our hearts are exposed and our character is shaped. The Lord wants our relationship with Him to be strengthened when we're in times of trouble. He wants to see how we'll react.

Many people only turn to the Lord when everything's going wrong; when it feels like the sky is falling down around them. They realize He's the most important thing after all and they should make Him their priority. In Matthew 13, Jesus talked about letting the wheat and the weeds grow up together until harvest. Rather than pulling up the weeds, the sower allowed them to grow up together at the same time. We believe this is happening in the world at the moment; the weeds are growing stronger but so is the wheat.

We can learn a lot through the truth of the scripture, *"Seek first the kingdom of God and his righteousness, and all these things shall be added to you."* (Matthew 6:33) This is the message of the hour: to seek after the Lord now. Go after God first. We need to get our thinking realigned with the reality of heaven because the Lord wants to prepare us for that which is to come. He is looking for His faithful ones. We believe we need to reach the point of no longer being satisfied with barely making it to heaven, but to diligently seek Him, to buy the oil of intimacy and make Him our prize and purpose. Now is the time to be serious about drawing nearer to God; there is absolutely no time or incentive to be lukewarm. The five wise went somewhere the foolish did not go. Which group do you want to be in?

RESPONSE

Lord, how have I fallen asleep concerning the promise of your return? Make me ready to go and meet you. Show me your priorities for my life. Are there areas in my life that are out of balance — places where I'm self-centred and not Christ-centered?

Father, may I not grow weary and tired, but teach me how to live dependent on your leadership and unfailing love.

CHAPTER 3

Three Transformational Journeys

We believe supernatural encounters with our loving God are vital for Christians to lead a full life in Him. As we diligently seek the Lord to buy the oil of intimacy, we meet Him in wonderful ways. But we've noticed it doesn't end there. In fact, intimacy with Him opens us up to new vision and opportunity to give His love away.

In 1994, the Holy Spirit mightily impacted our little church near Toronto Airport. On January 20th that year we found out what it means in Acts 11 when it says, *"The Holy Spirit fell upon them."* (v. 15b) It was unexpected and completely wonderful. The faithful presence of the Holy Spirit has been visiting our congregations and meetings around the world ever since.

Since then the Lord has been leading us into deeper relationship with Him. Intimacy with God has changed us because we have a revelation of how good and kind He is. In turn, that revelation makes us want to spend more time with Him. Encountering and experiencing God brings Him ever closer. We've learned He's a loving Father — in fact, the perfect Father. What a powerful, life-changing reality that is — and one we want to give away to the whole world.

You see, when the River of God touches us the Holy Spirit wants to take us deeper in three different directions, each of which is a journey in itself. These three journeys transform our lives and enhance our intimacy with the Lord.

THE INWARD JOURNEY

The first is the inward journey, which is a journey of the heart. This journey is about *you*, about you getting healed up, equipped and growing in your faith and gifting.

The Father loves us with an amazing, everlasting love. Many of us are taught the *concept* that "God loves me" but this truth must make a journey from being knowledge in our heads to a revelation in our hearts. There's a vacuum in each of us that can't be satisfied by anything but His love. We're not ashamed to admit we really need Him. Our hearts need to be assured God is here for us and He cares. The inward journey is this journey of deep heart revelation. It's where we learn God really, really loves us not just for what we do, but for who we are — His sons and daughters.

As we encounter the Father's love He leads us into healing and freedom. Our hearts are often damaged by past hurts or painful experiences but God wants to set us free. There are some wonderful keys to deep healing and freedom. Soaking in the Father's love and letting it truly saturate you is a very healing process.

We also want to encourage you to embrace a lifestyle of forgiveness and repentance — it's so freeing! Forgiving someone is like taking a hook out of yourself that's been causing you pain and grief. Each one of us needs to continually forgive others for the hurts they've caused us. We also need to forgive ourselves. We even need to forgive God because we often blame Him for the things that go wrong (although, of course, He is always good). Forgiveness is one of the subjects that we both love to share and you can find out more in our book *Grace and Forgiveness*.[1] Every time we share this message, we see people physically and emotionally healed and lives completely transformed.

The Lord wants to reveal the God-given authority we can walk in. Each one of us is designed to live unashamed in the Father's love; to live as the sons and daughters He's created us to be. Can you imagine what it's like to walk around with your head held up in confidence, knowing that you are royalty, that you are chosen by the Creator and that you are deeply approved of? That's what we are all designed for!

THE UPWARD JOURNEY

The upward journey is a focus on Him. It's about falling in love with Jesus as your Saviour and worshipping in response to His overwhelming love. You can get to know and love God your Father and, yes, the Holy Spirit too. He is a wonderful trinitarian God. The great thing is the upward journey and the inward journey go hand in hand: *"We love Him because He first loved us."* (1 John 4:19)

What are the ways we respond to God's love for us? Through worship and adoration. Through remembering and acknowledging how wonderful He is. When Jesus was asked what the greatest commandment is He replied:

"'You shall love the Lord your God with all your heart, with all
your soul, and with all your mind.' This is the first and great commandment. And the second is like it: 'You shall love your neighbor
as yourself.' On these two commandments hang all the Law and
the Prophets." (Matthew 22:37–40)

There's always more of His love to discover. We can constantly
press in and go deeper in Him. As we venture on the inward
journey where our hearts are inspired, our natural response is
to look upwards and respond in praise and thankfulness for
who He is and what He's revealing to us.

Thankfulness is an incredible tool for the upward journey.
As we remember who He is and the ways He's blessed us, we
lift our eyes off our earthly circumstances and begin to focus
on Heaven. When we see earthly problems from a heavenly
perspective they look much smaller. Every day, try declaring
things for which you're grateful to God. Search deep in your
heart for those revelations that inspire true thankfulness in
you. It may take a little while to get going but you won't be disappointed. Eventually, your whole attitude toward life will change
and your worship will go to new depths. Studies have shown
that practising gratitude makes people live longer, happier and
more fulfilled lives.[2]

THE OUTWARD JOURNEY

Finally, the outward journey is about reaching out to the people
around us. This is the adventure of the Great Commandment
combined with the Great Commission; loving others as we love

ourselves and making disciples of all nations (see Matthew 22:39; 28:19). When we embark on the outward journey, we choose to live for Him, work for Him, glorify Him in all we do and love others because of Him.

Ideally, the outward journey is a response to both the inward journey and the upward journey. All three work together. How can we share God's love and disciple others if we're not experiencing His love and growing ourselves? We won't find fulfillment if we only work on our own issues (*Inward*). If we worship and pray regularly (*Upward*) without ministering, we'll always feel we're lacking something. People often feel very satisfied and fulfilled when they're helping others (*Outward*), but to do that long-term you must be replenished yourself. To give love and life away, we must be continuously filled up so we're ministering out of overflow and abundance.

THE DIVINE ROMANCE

Imagine these three journeys as connecting lakes. Each of them produces movement in the others so the water doesn't stagnate. A stagnant body of water with no outward flow becomes stale, and as algae grows it turns into an inhospitable environment for other life forms. As we respond to the inward and upward journeys, there must be an outflow where God uses us to minister to and love on other people.

There are many ways that we can serve and help others. Loving people, caring for them and winning people to Christ are all vital to partnering with God for harvest. God wants to use every one of us in these days of amazing harvest. And every one of us has a ministry to be a blessing. The lost really are lost and God is not willing that any should perish, but that all should come to repentance and come to know Him as Saviour and Lord (2 Peter 3:9). He doesn't need us really, but He chooses us. He longs for us to be harvesters and disciples. His heart is for us to be passionate about evangelism, mission, and reaching a lost and dying world with His amazing, redeeming love; seeing His Kingdom come and changing hearts one soul at a time.

However, we can't neglect the upward journey of loving Him nor the inward journey of being healed up enough to love ourselves. We've found the reason some Christians find it so difficult to love others is because they haven't fully fallen in love with the Lord or they don't love themselves. We're convinced we need to be filled up with His presence. Without an overflow of life, love and passion, other people can merely become a "project".

The divine romance of the upward journey is such a powerful part of what the Lord is doing. Consider the Kingdom of Heaven from the perspective of the Bride and the Bridegroom. Jesus is calling the nations to Himself. He's calling you to love Him as your best friend as you respond to His love for you. The only problem in the Ephesian church was that they had left their first love (Revelations 2:4). Forgiving yourself and others will help you to be loving again.

RESPONSE

Thank you, Father, that you have chosen me. I surrender and commit my life to you. Help me to see myself as you do; awaken your love in me. I desire to love you with my whole heart, and from the overflow. Help me give to others the love I freely receive from you. Holy Spirit, I pray that you'll lead, guide and teach me in all that I do.

Forgiveness Prayer

Father, I choose to forgive those who have hurt me and sinned against me. I give them the gift of my unconditional forgiveness, with no strings attached. They owe me nothing. I trust you God to turn it all for good (Romans 8:28).

Lord, I also forgive myself for my own failures and mistakes. I let go of it all. I trust in the grace of the Lord Jesus Christ.

CHAPTER 4

Building Intimacy

You may have read the previous chapter and thought, "That's great. But what practical ways can I build intimacy with the Lord?" Whether you find yourself in a dry place which seems devoid of the life of the Holy Spirit or you're in a place where the Lord is pouring out His presence, there are some very straightforward ways you can develop an intimate relationship with the Father.

GETTING HUNGRY

Firstly, it helps to build a hunger for more of the Lord. Did you know you can ask Him to make you even hungrier? We don't have to wait until we're in a dry place to be hungry for more of God. In fact, we've found the more we encounter the wonderful presence of the Holy Spirit, the more we desire Him.

In 1991, we moved from pastoring in Stratford, Ontario to pastor our new church in Toronto. We quickly became deeply involved in the practical aspects of running a church. Shortly after this we realized we'd run dry through ministering daily, counseling, healing and working through deliverance with people. Yes, they were growing and maturing, but it took several years for them to become relatively free inside. Battling the darkness, rather than dispelling it with light, had become our focus. And it was wearing us out.

Benny Hinn visited our area in September 1992, and we knew we had to attend his meetings. We were longing for the power and manifest presence of the Holy Spirit and we desperately needed refreshing. What we saw at those meetings made us remember we have a very big God. The lame walked, the blind received their sight, deaf ears were opened and about 1,000 people came to Christ.

Powerfully touched by the experience, we said to God, "That's what we want, Lord."

And we felt Him say, "If you're serious, I want you to do two things: give me your mornings, and interact with others who are anointed."

We were serious, so in October 1992 we cancelled our engagements and began giving our mornings to the Lord. We worshipped, studied the Bible, prayed, read inspirational books and spent time with Him every morning for a year and a half. It was easier said than done, but we prioritized it. Weeks and months along the way, it became our absolute joy. We had fallen back in love with Jesus. We had returned to our first love. The more we pursued Him, the more He filled us up and the more we desired to be with Him.

We also invited guest speakers to our church. Their denominational affiliation didn't matter. If we heard they were anointed and used by God, we wanted them to come, hoping we could learn from them.

Around mid-August 1993, Marc Dupont[1] prophesied a mighty outpouring like Niagara Falls was coming. This was followed by equally strong prophecies from Stacey Campbell[2] and Larry Randolf.[3] In the previous year and a half we'd been stirring up our hunger for the Lord, so these prophecies made us even hungrier. In November 1993, we took a trip to experience the outpouring in Argentina, and this further ignited a passion for revival in our hearts. It was a prayer of impartation from Claudio Freidzon,[4] a leader in the Argentinian revival, that changed everything for us.

When we heard Randy Clark[5] had also been touched by the Holy Spirit, we asked him to speak at our church in January 1994. His first meeting on January 20th was a day that would go down in history. Randy shared his testimony, telling how the Holy Spirit had taken him from deep discouragement and replaced his hunger with fire. When he invited our little Thursday night group to receive more, heaven opened and glory came down. We were all changed that night! What did it look like? Chaos! There were bodies everywhere as we were physically overwhelmed by the Holy Spirit. We fell to the floor, with some laughing and some crying in the Spirit.

God will meet your hunger when you're serious about pursuing Him. When we first decided to give our mornings to the Lord in 1992, we had no clue it would lead us into a revival in Toronto that would endure for decades to come. We were just following His call to fall in love with Him. He's calling you in the same way, right now, to fall deeper in love with Him. It might not look the same as with us; the Lord does something different in all of us. But as you fuel that desire to be with Jesus, He will prepare your heart for what He wants to do.

We want to encourage you to go to places that will stir up

your faith, hunger and passion regularly. That might mean finding anointed speakers or conferences, or even following the Holy Spirit to an outpouring in another country, like when we went to Argentina. Those meetings really changed us both, as we were gloriously overwhelmed in the anointing. When we invest our time in the priorities of God, it will never be a waste. *"But seek first the kingdom of God and His righteousness, and all these things shall be added to you."* (Matthew 6:33)

HEARING GOD'S VOICE

When we planted churches in Stratford and Toronto, Ontario, we wanted to see God work in the lives of our church family. God led us to connect with Mark Virkler who had received an amazing revelation of how to hear God's voice.[6] Mark would describe himself as an analytical, rational and logical thinker. He wanted to know how to hear God's voice for himself but when he asked more naturally intuitive or creative people all they could say was that hearing God's voice is just something that "you know that you know that you know." This didn't satisfy Mark so he gave a year of his life to learning how to hear God's voice. God revealed four very straightforward steps based out of Habakkuk 2:1–2. They are:

1. Quiet yourself down
2. Fix your eyes on Jesus
3. Tune into spontaneous thoughts
4. Write it down

Mark has so much wisdom and insight into this topic, there's no point in us repeating it all here. He has a number of amazing books, video teachings, manuals and other resources to help you grow in communion with the Lord every day. If you've never heard this teaching before, we believe it's a vital tool for every Christian to really draw near to the Lord. Hearing God's voice was one of the keys for us that helped us to step into much deeper intimacy with the Lord.

When I (John) first learned to hear the voice of God, I thought, "It can't be this easy!" I'd get serious before the Lord and ask Him what He wanted to say. He'd reply,

"I love you, my son."

Then I'd say, "That's great, but what do you want to say next?"

And He would say, "I love you, my son."

That would happen six or more times and I began to think it was getting a bit corny. But actually that was what I needed to hear. God's kingdom is the Kingdom of Love. As I heard Him speak to me, I began to know more of His heart for me and for others. The things of God are childlike, aren't they?

SOAKING

Soaking is time immersed in God's presence. No petitions, no agenda, just being with Him. In the past Christians have called it "contemplative prayer" or "tarrying". It's about simply resting and waiting in the presence of the Holy Spirit and letting Him fill you up. Often people listen to calm, peaceful music that welcomes the presence of God as they soak. Usually we lie down or perhaps sit in a comfortable chair where we feel relaxed. Personally, we find that soaking allows God's presence to wash over us.

A prominent belief in the church is that we need to *do*

more; pray more, share the gospel more, read the Word more. Soaking is the opposite of that because it's about *being* before *doing*. It's where we give up our striving and trying to make things happen on our own and we allow the Lord to come close and meet with us. But soaking isn't a passive waiting. There is faith involved. When you soak you're actively positioning yourself in the presence of God with an expectation that something is going to happen. You're allowing Him into your heart to speak to you at a much deeper level. As you become more filled with the Holy Spirit, that's when the desire to give Him away to others is born. This is what it means to minister to others out of the overflow and abundance you've first received.

Hearing the voice of God is a key part of actively soaking in God's presence as it stimulates your relationship and personal communication with the Lord. When you know how to hear His voice you can tune in to what He's saying to you as you relax and soak.

When we're ministering, we've discovered continuing to pray for people and soak them in the presence of God has a dramatic effect. Often people fall down under the power of the Holy Spirit. But that's just the beginning; it's when they stay on the floor and allow God to work in them that deep healing or blessing happens. I remember several times when Carol would pray over people for four hours or more, pouring the anointing into them and soaking them in His power. It changed their lives forever because they met with God in such a deep way.

THE 10 MINUTE WORSHIP REVOLUTION

Recently, I (Carol) experienced some quite serious colon problems that lasted two years. I was constantly exhausted, dehydrated and discouraged but the worst part was that I couldn't feel the presence of God as I normally do. The Holy Spirit was still there when I ministered, but I didn't feel His presence for myself. I cannot begin to explain how devastating this was for me. I simply live for intimacy with our wonderful Trinitarian God.

After bad reports from multiple doctors in Toronto, I eventually headed to Germany on the recommendation of good friends. I spent time in a Christian community which combines high quality medical care with constant prayer and ministry. Miraculously, a doctor there discovered a tiny parasite that was causing havoc in my body. They were able to deal with it; the colitis cleared up and my strength returned, but I was still struggling to sense God's presence.

Then John and I met Dr. Arne Elsen, a medical doctor with an incredible healing ministry in Hamburg in the North of Germany. After becoming a follower of Jesus, Dr. Elsen was struck by the instruction in 1 Thessalonians 5:17 to *"pray without ceasing."* He decided a practical way to do this was to use a timer to remind him every ten minutes to pray and worship God. Since then, Dr. Elsen discovered that praying and worshipping every ten minutes has been a wonderful key to physical healing for hundreds of people. We both decided to give it a go.

Well, using a timer reminding us to worship every ten minutes was certainly a challenge initially. It's so easy to get frustrated in life, like when you're driving and someone cuts you off. But then the buzzer goes off and it's time to worship the Lord. Having a ten minute worship timer helps us keep a positive mindset; it helps us stay connected with His presence amid the busyness of life.

After just a short while using this timer, I found that I could feel God's presence increasing intimacy again. It was wonderful. The worship timer has become like a lifeline for me and for so many others as well. We call it the *10 minute worship revolution*,[7] because it has really been a revolution.

Beni Johnson[8] from Bethel Church in Redding, California, recently shared with us she started using the timer after seeing the effect it had on me. Beni had been suffering with adrenal fatigue for three years and she was constantly tired and worn out. She'd tried medication from a naturopath but wasn't returning to her normal state of energy. After just two weeks of using the timer to remind her to worship every ten minutes, Beni woke up one morning and realized she was completely refreshed. All traces of adrenal fatigue were gone.

We've also seen an increased anointing for ministry and healing. As we worship, God's presence permeates the atmosphere. He's the one doing the healing, but we've noticed as we worship over people, we're welcoming more of His presence to come and heal.

A TEAM EFFORT

Alongside spending time one-on-one with the Lord, when we get together with others the group dynamic encourages us to go deeper. If you want to pursue intimacy then why not join in with a small group of like-minded people? You can worship, pray, intercede, meditate on the Word and soak together. When intimacy with the Lord is the goal of the whole group, you can help motivate one another to press in. Breakthrough can sometimes be a little more difficult when you're on your own with your own thoughts to distract you.

RESPONSE

Holy Spirit, increase a hunger in my heart for intimacy with you. I desire to live in unity with you, continually knowing and hearing the thoughts of your heart.

Father, thank you that you sent your Son for me so that I may know you as He did. I pray for my ears to be open to hear your voice and for the eyes of my heart to see you, so that I may know you more.

CHAPTER 5

Birth Pains

It's important to be ready and embrace a lifestyle of intimacy with the Lord. Nobody knows the day or the hour of Jesus' return. In fact, the exact End Time scenario has been designed to be obscure.

Having said that, the Bible was written with many signs and clues so we can estimate the End Time seasons. The first three key passages to consider are Matthew 24, Mark 13 and Luke 21. Take some time yourself to read and meditate on these chapters where Jesus speaks of His return. Let's take a look at Matthew 24:

> "And you will hear of wars and rumors of wars. See that you are not troubled; for all these things must come to pass, but the end is not yet. For nation will rise against nation, and kingdom against kingdom. And there will be famines, pestilences, and earthquakes in various places. All these are the beginning of sorrows." (vv. 6–8)

Jesus said all the things listed in this passage will come to pass, but the end is not yet. In verse eight, the New King James Version uses the word "sorrow", but interestingly, many other translations use the phrase "birth pains" which is what the original Greek text says.

John became a father during the days when husbands weren't welcome in the delivery room, so he knew very little about what goes on during labor. He asked me recently to tell him about birth pains. I explained they start off mildly but increase both in frequency and intensity to the point of desperation when you really know the baby is coming whether you're ready or not. There's no stopping it. Jesus said when we see signs of these "birth pains" we know the end is beginning, whether we're prepared or not.

In Charles Dicken's *A Tale of Two Cities*[1] there's a poignant phrase, "*It was the best of times, it was the worst of times...*" We believe this is true for the time we're living in right now. But our culture teaches us not to listen to things we perceive as negative. We choose to listen to what we want to hear, which is that things will only improve and tomorrow will be better than today. Yet the Bible clearly tells us that the End Times scenario is going to be like birth pains, starting off mildly but increasing both in frequency and intensity. If we're wise, we'll listen and pay attention so we're able to respond accordingly.

BOILING THE FROG

When tragedies strike repeatedly and with increasing frequency, we can unknowingly become conditioned to it and desensitized. Consider the old adage of boiling the frog. Don't try this at home, but apparently, if you put a frog into hot water, it will immediately jump out. However, if you put the frog into cool water and gradually increase the temperature to boiling point, the frog won't jump out but will cook to death. Similarly, we believe we've slowly been conditioned to the birth pains of the End Times and are taking little notice of the increasing calamities around us.

The Twentieth Century hit like a bomb. The rapid development of automobiles, airplanes, radio, television and movies, the atomic bomb and computers; alongside the two World Wars and the Great Depression, it really made people question when Christ would return. Others began to doubt the existence of God. Now we are into the Third Millennium AD.

Right at the beginning of this millennium a major catastrophe occurred. On September 11, 2001, the World Trade Centers were destroyed by terrorists intentionally flying an aircraft to crash into them. We were in Brazil at the time and received a phonecall telling us the news. We knew the world would never be the same again.

Following September 11, the war in Afghanistan began and then the war in Iraq. In the midst of that the SARS epidemic[2] broke out in many parts of the world, including Toronto. There were major threats of bird flu and swine flu. Reports from the World Health Organization suggested we were very close to experiencing worldwide epidemics similar to, or worse than, the 1910s when tens of millions died.[3] In 2004 there were more terrorist attacks on trains in Spain, and in 2005 on subways in London, England. And then, in 2008, the economy crashed.

Previously, in August 2007, I (John) was at RIVERcamp, a family event focused on the Holy Spirit. On the final night of the camp, the Lord woke me up at 7:00 AM sharp with these words booming in my ears, "Global economic catastrophe."

Wide awake and shocked, I asked, "Lord, what are you saying?" I questioned Him, "When, Lord?" I felt like He was saying that it would start in January 2008. We told several of our friends and in early 2008 we even shared about it on CBN television with Pat Robertson. Sure enough, the crash came, in September 2008, from which we still have not fully recovered.

Many nations such as Portugal, Italy, Ireland, Greece and Spain are left seriously struggling. We don't know what will happen with this economic disaster. America is in a crisis with a serious government debt of 17 trillion dollars. A trillion is a million millions. If we use the concept of time, it helps us to grasp the severity of this debt. One million seconds is about 12 days ago. One billion seconds is about 31 years ago. Contrast that to a trillion seconds which is about 31,000 years ago! How does the richest country on earth get into trillions of dollars of debt? It will take a lot to recover from such a huge deficit. When the Lord used the word "catastrophe" when He spoke to me that morning, He wasn't exaggerating.

Meanwhile, violence is increasing around the world. In 2010 the Arab Spring[4] started with an uprising in Tunisia, soon spreading to Egypt, Libya, Iran and Jordan. Seventeen Arab and Muslim nations have been affected by this and it continues as we write, as Syria is torn apart by civil war and Egypt is again in turmoil.

Likewise, there are tragedies at home. At the end of 2012, in Connecticut, 20 elementary school children were killed in the second deadliest school shooting in United States' history.[5] In early 2013, the Boston Marathon was bombed and innocent spectators were killed or injured.[6] In July 2013, there were two disastrous train wrecks in Spain and in Switzerland, then a tragic bus accident in Italy, and the list goes on.

We certainly want to keep aware of all that's going on, to avoid being like that frog in boiling water!

SIGNS IN THE EARTH

Along with economic disaster and increased violence, the whole earth is being shaken up. There are signs throughout the planet of change and destruction, as indicated in Matthew 24.

Indonesia experienced a devastating tsunami in 2004 when approximately 200,000 people were killed.[7] In 2005, Hurricane Katrina destroyed New Orleans. In 2011, Japan experienced a tsunami which left almost 20,000 dead[8] and continues to contaminate the oceans with deadly radiation. All these are birth pains and travail in the earth. We're not implying God is causing these things to happen, and we're certain His hope is for us to run to Him during these times.

In 2010, Eyjafjallajökull, an erupting volcano in Iceland, caused havoc all over Europe. Aircrafts and passengers were grounded all over the world. We learned through research that the erupting volcano was close to the Laki volcanic fissure in southern Iceland. It erupted in 1783 for over eight months, causing ash clouds to block sunlight and prevent crops from growing. Famine in Europe resulted and so the eruption probably contributed to the French Revolution.[9] Remember the classic quote attributed to Marie Antoinette, *"Let them eat cake"*? While it is debated who actually said it, it came in response to the starving people's plight.

The BP oil spill in the Gulf of Mexico in 2010 was the worst in history.[10] Almost five million barrels of oil were spilled and BP weren't able to cap it for three months. What devastating effects has that had on our planet and wildlife? The 2011 floods in Australia covered an area as large as France and Germany, wiping out thousands of homes, wildlife, cattle and crops.[11] Two years before that, 173 were killed in uncontrollable fires that were burning because of the lack of rain. About 400 fires started on one day, spreading across 1,100,000 acres and causing $4.4 billion worth of damage. It was called "Black Saturday" and is the eighth deadliest bushfire ever recorded.[12] Winters have been increasingly worse in Europe. I (John) remember seeing a satellite image of the British Isles completely covered in snow from top to bottom.[13] The UK is not prepared for that as we are in Canada! In 2011, an earthquake struck the South Island of New Zealand, killing 185 people.[14] The government declared a state of national emergency for two months.

A while ago I, (John) was sharing this message in Stratford, Ontario. While I was speaking, the town center of Goodrich, just less than an hour away, was taken out by a tornado. Millions of dollars worth of damage was done, with one person killed.[15] It's incredible; one minute the town is there, the next minute it's a pile of rubble. It was like a gigantic vacuum cleaner swept through the middle of Goodrich.

In North Carolina, Shaw University was devastated by a tornado in 2011.[16] In just four days, over 200 tornadoes struck in the southeast of the US, killing 316 people.[17] Then we heard reports of fires in Texas, Arizona and California. Forty percent of the city of Slave Lake in Canada was burned to the ground due to uncontrollable fires.[18] It couldn't be stopped. Then the floods came in Mississippi, Georgia and Manitoba; all of which destroyed many urban and rural areas. In October 2012, Hurricane Sandy swept across the Caribbean and the East Coast of North America, leaving about 150 dead[19] and billions of dollars worth of damage. New York City experienced devastating flooding, fires and power shortages. Then in June and July of 2013, two major Canadian cities, Calgary and Toronto, were totally flooded by torrential rain, causing billions of dollars of damage. It had never happened before.[20]

Meanwhile, there are famines all over North Africa creating untold human suffering.

Jesus describes another sign of the end as *"the sea and the waves roaring."* (Luke 21:25) This is very clear in situations like the earthquake in Fukushima, Japan, in March 2011. With a magnitude of 9.0, it became one of the worst natural disasters ever, causing a tsunami over 25 feet high in some places. The wave hit a nuclear power station and cut the power supply and the backup supply. Three nuclear reactors couldn't be cooled, so there was a meltdown, resulting in radioactive material leaking into the ocean. The sea and waves roared.

Do we need to look around and ask God what is going on in our world? Hebrews 12 tells us everything that can be shaken will be shaken, so only that which cannot be shaken will remain. Things around us can seem dark and bleak, and doomed to get darker. This is the worst of times, but remember, it is also the best of times and we're choosing to be hopeful. The coming Wedding of Christ and His Bride is more sure than tomorrow's sunrise. We are so thankful that on Christ the Solid Rock we stand, when all other ground is sinking sand.

WILL YOU LOVE HIM AT ALL TIMES?

Amid tragedy and disaster, there is positive testimony. We had a friend staying in Port-au-Prince, Haiti, in January 2010 when the devastating earthquake hit. Christina was in a pastor's house, sleeping. After the earthquake, she managed to climb out of the rubble with her purse and two other items: her passport and a bottle of water. That was all she had for three days.

Frequent aftershocks caused debris to fall everywhere. People were too afraid to go near buildings so they stayed in the fields. Christina said despite the chaos, something quite wonderful happened. Haiti is known as the Voodoo capital of the world where Satan is worshipped, yet the Prime Minister called for a week of prayer, worship and preaching. For an entire week, one million people gathered together[22] 24/7. Thousands were saved, even Voodoo priests.

Testimonies like that are fantastic. But does Jesus want a Bride that only wants Him as a last resort? We don't know what will happen next, but we do know when there's nothing left, people come running to God. The test is on, and we believe He's saying, "I want to know if you love me in the best of times, not only in the worst of times."

In the book of Revelation, John is shown a vision:

> After these things I looked, and behold, a great multitude which no one could number, of all nations, tribes, peoples, and tongues, standing before the throne and before the Lamb, clothed with white robes, with palm branches in their hands, and crying out with a loud voice, saying, "Salvation belongs to our God who sits on the throne, and to the Lamb!" All the angels stood around the throne and the elders and the four living creatures, and fell on their faces before the throne and worshiped God, saying:

> "Amen! Blessing and glory and wisdom,
> Thanksgiving and honor and power and might,
> Be to our God forever and ever.
> Amen."

Then one of the elders answered, saying to me, "Who are these arrayed in white robes, and where did they come from?"

And I said to him, "Sir, you know."

So he said to me, "These are the ones who come out of the great tribulation, and washed their robes and made them white in the blood of the Lamb. Therefore they are before the throne of God, and serve Him day and night in His temple. And He who sits on the throne will dwell among them. They shall neither hunger anymore nor thirst anymore; the sun shall not strike them, nor any heat; for the Lamb who is in the midst of the throne will shepherd them and lead them to living fountains of waters. And God will wipe away every tear from their eyes." (7:9–17)

There's going to be a huge harvest of souls coming out of the Great Tribulation, yet we are convinced there's another number of people who are so in love with the Bridegroom He'll spare that Bride from the Tribulation. The opportunity to be part of the Bride is open to every believer.

This is mentioned in Revelation 3, for the faithful church of Philadelphia.

"Because you have kept My command to persevere, I also will keep you from the hour of trial which shall come upon the whole world, to test those who dwell on the earth." (3:10)

Would you like to be kept from the hour of trial? We know we certainly would.

RESPONSE

God, help me to remain faithful to you. How can I prepare myself for your great return? How can you use me as your vessel in preparing your Bride?

Holy Spirit, fan the flame on the inside of me, that I may be fully aware of you in all that I do.

CHAPTER 6

Revival is Spreading

There are many tragedies on the earth but heaven's victories are also multiplying. The wheat and the weeds are maturing as they grow together. There is good news in Habakkuk 2:14: *"For the earth will be filled with the knowledge of the glory of the Lord, as the waters cover the sea."* This is not just a revelation about God, but a promise that the knowledge of the Lord's glory is going to fill the whole earth. We are excited about that! This is a reality that's happening before our eyes.

One hundred years ago, the Christian world was very different. For example, Asia was spiritually different. There were almost no Christians in Korea. Today, up to 50% of South Koreans claim to be Christian.[1] There are huge churches thriving in South Korea, including one that was for many years the largest church in the world, pastored by Dr. David Yonggi Cho, with 800,000 members.[2]

We went on our first mission trip to Indonesia in 1980. We were told that Indonesia was the largest Muslim country on the planet at 97% Muslim and 3% other religions. Christianity was perhaps just 1–2%. We were business people at the time, wanting to give our testimony and see if we could raise money to help the people there, but they thought we were evangelists from Canada.

When we arrived, we discovered they'd planned meetings all over the place, including a three day crusade, which just floored me. We were stretched well beyond our limit, but while we were ministering, leading meetings and small groups, we learned the Lord could indeed use us. God moved and it was amazing. And the people loved on us so much that we came home in tears. On the plane we said, "We can't give our lives to business anymore; we have to go into the ministry." (At that time. we didn't know that the Lord was sending us to Carol's hometown of Stratford.) We have heard that unofficially, the percentage of Christians in Indonesia has risen amazingly to about 30%.

China sees around 30,000 people become followers of Jesus every day. It has continued on for over 30 years. That's almost one million per month. We saw a video[3] about the 10/40 window recently which states clearly that in ten years time, China will be a Christian nation. The 10/40 window refers to nations that are between 10 and 40 degrees north of the equator, including much of the eastern hemisphere. These are places that were described in 1990 as having the least access to the gospel on the planet. But today revival is raging in China.

In 1993 we went to Argentina to experience the revival there. We were wonderfully touched by the Holy Spirit. If we hadn't gone there, we honestly don't know where we would be today. In Argentina we received a powerful impartation, and it's been 20 years from the time of writing since revival hit our church in Toronto. It's still fantastic! Revival remains in Argentina and in Brazil too. C Peter Wagner said that the center of revival has moved to Brazil, where it is blazing.[4]

Randy Clark visited a Brazilian Baptist church several years ago when there were around 300 people in the congregation. He returned for a second visit two to three years later. The church had grown to 2,000. The following two years after that, he went again to find it had grown to 10,000. Then recently, he visited again and was astonished to find the church had planted 23 local churches and overall was 30,000 strong. That is unbelievable growth in just six or seven years. Are we prepared for growth like that? Do we even expect growth like that in our churches?

As the darkness is becoming darker, the light is becoming brighter. We need to get ready for revival. We believe we're going to see a huge harvest on both sides of the coming of the Lord for His Bride.

In 2005, we were in Colombia for a pastors conference. The day after we arrived we left the hotel to go for a walk. Suddenly, a van came screeching up behind us. It pulled up and three big guys jumped out. I (John) immediately thought, "Oh my gosh, they're kidnapping us." But it turned out that they were our bodyguards.

The said to us, "What are you doing? Get in the car please, this is too dangerous." So we were taken back to the hotel. We hadn't realized it wasn't safe to go anywhere without at least one of our bodyguards.

One of the bodyguards even had a gun. Amusingly, Carol started gesturing as if she was shooting him with a gun of anointing in the Spirit. He would be standing against the wall, watching carefully, talking into his radio and doing his job. Then Carol would look over at him, gesture to shoot him in the Spirit with a bang, and he would hit the wall and slide down to the floor. The most hilarious thing was, later she asked him,

"Whose gun do you prefer? Yours or mine?"

"I'd rather have yours," he said.

I was back in Colombia two years ago with Jerry Anderson, and I was amazed at the transformation. Jerry and his team are part of La Red, an organisation that teaches principles and values based on the book of Proverbs, to businessmen, schools, and the military in the nation. At one time, Colombia's military were known as thugs. They would come to rob, loot and rape. Entire towns hated the military for what they did and who they were. Now, through encountering the truth of God's Word, things are changing. There was a completely different atmosphere.

We spent one afternoon with General Perez, the second in command of the Air Force. Apparently, over 300,000 military service personnel have been taught the values and principles in the book of Proverbs.[5] Through the power of biblical values and principles, and the knowledge of right and wrong, amazing transformation has taken place, praise the Lord! What an amazing opportunity to bring the Father's love and welcome the power of the Holy Spirit in a place which so desperately needs it. Colombia and other areas of Latin America are now on fire for Christ.

And most amazing of all, the gospel is also spreading through the Middle East. I visited Turkey for the first time in November 2011. I went to four cities and was blown away by the people I met and the stories they told me. A year before my trip there, I met a man who was involved with work in Iran. He told me there was a revival in Iran. He estimated that about one million Iranians were born again Christians because God had supernaturally appeared to them in dreams and visions. This was certainly confirmed when I was in Turkey.

In every single meeting there was a little huddle of Iranians translating the message to one another in Farsi, their native language. They had fled to Turkey as refugees. Everywhere I went I'd see another group of them, and I was desperate to talk to them. I had to find out, so I asked, "I heard there are a million Iranians out of 70 million that have been born again. Is that correct?"

"No," they said. "There are at least two million!"

Then we read Joel Rosenberg's book, *Inside the Revolution: How the Followers of Jihad, Jefferson, and Jesus are Battling to Dominate the Middle East and Transform the World.* Rosenberg is a believer who spent about 20 years in the Middle East while working with the New York Times. He said that not one million, not two, but he believed seven million Iranians have had a supernatural revelation of Jesus in Iran.

He tells the true story about two Christians driving through the mountains of Iran with a car full of Bibles, trying to smuggle them from Turkey:

> "Suddenly, their steering wheel jammed and they had to slam on the brakes to keep from driving off the side of the road. When they looked up, they saw an old man knocking on their windows and asking if they had the books.
>
> 'What books?' They asked.
>
> 'The books about Jesus.' The old man replied. He went on to explain that an angel recently came to him in a vision and told him about Jesus. Later he found out that everyone in the village had had the same vision. They were all brand new followers of Jesus, but they did not know what to do next. Then the old man had a dream in which Jesus told him to go down the mountain and wait for someone for bring books that would explain how to

be a Christian. He obeyed, and suddenly two men with a car full of Bibles came to a stop right in front of him." (pp. 387–388)[6]

There are countless incredible stories like this one. There is revival all over the earth today.

RESPONSE

Father, I thank you that your Spirit still moves today. I pray for revival in my city and among the nations.

Teach me Holy Spirit how to be carrier of your presence, and how to demonstrate your Kingdom in power and love. Father, please give me a personal revival, so I can pour it out on others.

CHAPTER 7

The Importance of Israel

When considering the End Times it's important to think about the role of Israel. In Matthew, Mark and Luke, Jesus points to a fig tree. He says, *"Now learn this parable from the fig tree: When its branch has already become tender and puts forth leaves, you know that summer is near."* (Matthew 24:32; Mark 13:28; Luke 21:29 NIV). Israel is represented by the fig tree. When we see certain signs within Israel, we know the Kingdom is near.

Some want to tread carefully or ignore the subject of Israel altogether. But let us emphasise that Israel is there not because of their righteousness, but because of the promises God made to Abraham, Isaac, Jacob and David. The Arab people, bless them, are no different to you and I. They are Gentiles, as we are. Our heart is for them to turn to Christ and to be saved, as it is for all the nations. But scripture makes it clear that in the last days God will restore His land to the Jewish people.

When we read Ezekiel 36 and 37 we clearly see that God says to Israel at the time of the end, "I'm going to restore you to the land that I promised you." (See Ezekiel 36:22–28)

In the valley of dry bones He asks Ezekiel,

"'Son of man, can these bones live?'

So I answered, 'O LORD GOD, You know.'" (37:3)

Ezekiel was trying to be a man of faith. The Lord told him to prophesy to the bones and as he did, he saw them come together and stand up to become a great army. *"These bones are the whole house of Israel."* (37:11a)

THREE PROPHECIES FULFILLED

Another key reason we need to look at Israel is because two of three major prophecies concerning Christ's return are about the nation of Israel.

Firstly, it was prophesied that before the return of Jesus, Israel had to become a nation once again. Jesus speaks of a fig tree blossoming as a sign of the end (Matthew 24:32–34; Mark 13:28–30; Luke 21:29). Israel is referred to as a fig tree throughout scripture, so we can understand that Jesus is saying that when we see Israel blossoming it is a sign of His near return. These scriptures also relate to Ezekiel 36 and 37 where the Lord promises to regather Israel. Israel was indeed regathered. In 1948 when I (John) was just 7 years old Israel became a nation once again.

Secondly, it was prophesied that Jerusalem would again become a Jewish city in preparation for the restoration of the temple. In Luke 21:24 Jesus says, *"And Jerusalem will be trampled* (or occupied) *by Gentiles until the times of the Gentiles are fulfilled."* Jesus also spoke about the destruction of the temple in Matthew 24:2 when he said, *"Assuredly, I say to you, not one stone shall be left here upon another, that shall not be thrown down."* In AD 70 the Roman army destroyed Jerusalem and began the scattering of the nation of Israel. This was a time of great wrath upon Israel. But this isn't the end of the story.

Both Daniel and Paul talk about how in the End Times the antichrist will put a stop to temple worship and sacrifice (Daniel 9:27; 2 Thessalonians 2:3–4). From this we know that temple worship will be reinstated, before it can be halted again. Daniel and Paul saw that Jerusalem and its temple would be rebuilt. Similarly, in Luke 21:24 Jesus addressed both the pending destruction of the city and the end-times restoration. The restoration of Jerusalem has already happened, in 1967 Jerusalem became a Jewish city. In 1987 the Temple Institute was founded,[1] which seeks to educate and prepare the nation in practical ways for the restoration of the temple. In 2007 they announced the High Priest's crown was complete in readiness for the temple's restoration.[2]

The third prophecy is in the gospel of Matthew: *'And this gospel of the kingdom will be preached in all the world as a witness to all the nations, and then the end will come.'"* (v. 14) The gospel had not been preached in all nations until very recently. Now, thanks in part to increased access to the internet and TV around the world, revival is spreading through the nations of the world. There are Christians and churches in every nation. And the gospel has been preached in every country on earth, though not every individual has heard it yet.

Loren Cunningham, the founder of Youth With A Mission, was with us in Toronto in 2011. He said that by the year 2020, the Bible will be available in every known language and there will be a church not just in every nation, but in every known people group. 2020 is not far off.

All three of these prophecies have now been fulfilled. This shows us we're drawing nearer to the time Jesus will return.

We don't want to be thrust upon Jesus through fear and disaster. He longs to rescue everyone of course. But He also longs for a Bride that loves Him for who He is, and not for fear of what might happen to them if they don't follow Him. The bridal motivation must be one of pure and adoring love.

SIGNS IN THE MOON

In Luke 21 we read:

> "And there will be signs in the sun, in the moon, and in the stars; and on the earth distress of nations, with perplexity, the sea and the waves roaring; men's hearts failing them from fear and the expectation of those things which are coming on the earth, for the powers of the heavens will be shaken. Then they will see the Son of Man coming in a cloud with power and great glory. Now when these things begin to happen, look up and lift up your heads, because your redemption draws near." (vv. 25–28)

Jesus said there will be signs in the sun and moon. We have become aware of some very significant upcoming and unusual signs in the sun and moon.

In the years 2014 and 2015, there will be four consecutive lunar eclipses. Four lunar eclipses in a row, called a tetrad, are extremely rare;[3] they couldn't merely be by chance. Perhaps a partial eclipse or shadow eclipse, but not four total eclipses.

Ancient peoples called this type of eclipse a "blood moon".[4] This is because the moon is darkened by the earth's shadow and the only light seen is refracted through the earth's atmosphere, giving it a reddish hue. The astonishing fact is that these four eclipses all occur on Jewish feast days. Blood moons occur on the exact dates of the Passover (March/April) and Tabernacle Feasts (September/October) in 2014 and 2015.[5] These feasts are always on full moons but rarely on lunar eclipses.

I (John) found this fascinating and it got me searching on NASA's lunar website. I wondered when else there had been four consecutive lunar eclipses. What I found was amazing. In 1949 and 1950 we had the same scenario. Four blood moons in a row on Jewish feast days.[6] The first one occurred on the first Passover feast following the founding of Israel as a nation in May 1948.[7] 1949 was the first year of Israel's first elected government.

The next time this scenario happened was in 1967.[8] This was the same year of the six-day war against Israel which Israel won.[9] Jerusalem became a Jewish city for the first time since AD 70, as prophesied in Luke 21:24. In 1967 and 1968 there were four consecutive blood moons, once again occurring on the Passover and Tabernacle feasts. There is a pattern here. Four consecutive blood moon total lunar eclipses landing on the main Jewish feasts, three times in under 50 years. Previous to this, four total lunar eclipses in a row happening on Jewish feast days hasn't happened since 1492, when Columbus discovered America and Spain ordered all Jews to leave their country.

Here's the point; each time four consecutive blood moons have occurred there has been a significant war in the Middle East. We are not saying there is going to be a war in 2014 and 2015, because we have no way of knowing that. The truth is, we honestly don't know what will happen. However, we do know that Jesus warned us that there would be signs in the moon and blood moons have, in the past, meant trouble for Israel. We are convinced that this is serious enough to require your careful examination. You can research for yourself, Google the phrase "Catalog of Lunar Eclipses 2001–2100".

We feel so strongly about this that I (John) went to visit the General Consul of Israel in Toronto. I said, "Sir, we are here to honour you and support you, but I'm here because I believe there's a potentially serious security threat for the nation of Israel that you need to be aware of."

Seated on the edge of his chair, he listened intently as I told him about the lunar eclipses. I was with him for an hour and a half when we only originally had a 15 minute appointment. Israeli leaders are very concerned.

Another interesting event that seems significant to us, is that Iran is experiencing an unprecedented, sovereign revival and visitation of God. It is worrisome though, to see the Iranian government so opposed to the nation of Israel and to see them so committed to developing nuclear capabilities. In 2005, the president of Iran announced Israel should be "wiped out from the map".[10]

As I was discussing this with the General Consul, he leaned forward and said, "You do know that Israel cannot afford to allow Iran to get nuclear weapons, don't you?"

"I understand that," I said.

Something else to consider are signs in the sun. In March 2015, two weeks before the blood moon on Passover in April, there will be a total eclipse of the sun which will be visible from Europe and parts of the Middle East.[11] Luke states clearly that we should expect signs in the sun and the moon, and that month would give us both. (Luke 21:25–28) Again, we do not know what all this means, but we are told to be watchful. If it does point to war involving Iran and the Middle East, then it may be what Ezekiel 38 and 39 are referring to:

> "'You will come up against My people Israel like a cloud, to cover the land. It will be in the latter days that I will bring you against My land, so that the nations may know Me, when I am hallowed in you, O God, before their eyes.'" (38:16)

There is a lot to happen before Jesus returns to establish His kingdom. If there is a war in Israel in 2014 or 2015, and if God intervenes like He has done in the past, then it will be a game changer. Israel will waste no time in rebuilding their temple that was destroyed in AD 70. We'll see a whole different world emerging. It would be a time of great transition and I believe a time of great harvest. This is simply no time to be lukewarm toward the Lord.

RESPONSE

Father, please make me aware of what you are doing in this time. Help me to stand watch, eager and willing to partner with you. I want to fall in love with you, Jesus, not run to you out of fear of what might happen.

I choose to abide in you, and wholeheartedly I say "yes" to what you desire to do. Use me as your willing servant for your glory, God.

CHAPTER 8

A Fresh Outpouring

Amid the growing troubles in the earth, there are great global triumphs for God's Kingdom. It's clear the tension between the wheat and the weeds is going to increase more and more as they come into maturity. A lot of people don't want to listen to bad news but we think we need to pay attention to both sides of what is happening. Scripture clearly speaks of both the good and the bad.

We've noticed many churches around the world are experiencing pruning. Pruning is a hard process to go through; nobody likes to learn patience, but we need it. There was a time when we had a cherry tree in our back garden that really wasn't doing well. For two or three years, in spite of my care, it just seemed to be limping along. Eventually I (John) decided to seriously prune it. When Carol saw what I'd done, she said, "Oh my gosh, you cut it to nothing! Will it grow back from that?" But the next year that tree began to shoot up again and grew beautifully. The pruning helped it grow healthy.

This is true for the church too. It has to get to the place where the root system is more than able to provide nurture for the branches. If there are too many branches then the roots can't feed the whole tree, but if you reverse that then you get a very healthy tree.

We believe there's bountiful blessing just ahead. We believe God is getting us ready for an increased outpouring of His Spirit in different places all over the world. We're expecting the mightiest outpouring of the Holy Spirit anyone has ever seen. We believe it will eclipse what happened in the book of Acts because that's the way God works—the glory of the latter house will be greater than the former. We think there will be two aspects to this outpouring: firstly, that there will be a global harvest of souls and secondly, the preparation of the Bride for the Bridegroom.

People often ask me, "Well, when is this going to happen?" We've been expecting a greater wave in revival for the last 15 years or so. We know there's so much more to come than we've seen, as glorious as it is, and we're looking forward to it.

RESPONDING TO THE INVITATION

We've highlighted in this book that there's an invitation extended to all Christians to prepare for what's to come. Prepare to be the Bride of Christ and prepare to meet the Bridegroom. We're certain this call is becoming more urgent in these troubled times. With all that's happening in the earth, now is the time to buy the oil of intimacy. Now is the time to prepare for the marriage of Christ and His Bride.

"Let us rejoice and be glad and give him glory! For the wedding of the Lamb has come, and his bride has made herself ready." (Revelation 19:7 NIV)

Then the angel said to me, "Write this: Blessed are those who are invited to the wedding supper of the Lamb!" And he added, "These are the true words of God." (v. 9 NIV)

Notice that the bridegroom doesn't prepare the bride. She makes herself ready. He does not twist her arm and say, "Love me, or else." No. He's waiting for each of us to respond.

Allow us to challenge you: Do you feel low on the oil of intimacy? Were you once full and really in love with Jesus, your Bridegroom? Are you now focusing on the cares of this life? On your job, progressing in your career or watching the economy and making investments? Are you busy with your spouse, your kids and your home with little time for the Lord?

Are you lukewarm? Are you cold even? If the answer is yes to any of these questions, then we want to encourage you to humble yourself and get honest with the Lord. Invite Him back in to take first place. Invite Him to make you hungry and thirsty for Him once again.

'Buying' the oil of intimacy and preparing for the Lord's return is something you won't regret. Jesus, by the Holy Spirit, has made it so easy for us. You don't need to be rich to buy oil. You don't need to be intelligent to figure it out. You don't need to know the right people to get in on a good thing. All you need is the simple willingness to humble yourself and humbly return to having Him as Lord; to admit you've been wrong and you need a saviour to pay your debt.

If you're reading this and you've never invited Jesus to

come into your heart, to be your Saviour, then why not do that now and get started on the most wonderful journey of all? God is love and He will take you from your place of lack and fill you with His love that never fails. This sets us up for eternity, because we will spend eternity loving God.

Then make it your goal to buy the oil of intimacy. Learn what it means to soak in the Lord's presence. Learn to be a worshipper, a lover of God. Aim to get an abundant supply of extra oil so that you can love Him with all of your heart, soul, mind, and strength. Then you can go and love your neighbor as yourself and give away this revelation of the kingdom to people and friends around you.

And what if Jesus doesn't return for another 20 years, or 50 years? Something tells us you won't be disappointed when you choose to focus your life on time with Christ, our bridegroom King. In our opinion, we don't think there are 20 years left, considering all the signs and fulfilled prophecy. And what if he returned next year unexpectedly?

This is certainly no time to be lukewarm. This is not the time to be low on oil. The hour is late and things are happening, whether the Bride is ready or not. *"Behold, the bridegroom is coming."* (Matthew 25:6)

RESPONSE

Holy Spirit help me not to become complacent.

Jesus, thank you that I was created to love you and to be loved by you. How can I live a life of increasing passion for you? As I draw near to your heart, may I fall deeper in love with you. Come, Holy Spirit, and fill my lamp with oil.

Meditate on Ezekiel 38–39, and Matthew 25:1–13.

Endnotes

CHAPTER 1

1 Matthew 25:12. See both http://www.blueletterbible.org/lang/lexicon/lexiconcfm?strongs=G1492 &t=NKJV Retrieved: September 07, 2013 and http://www.biblestudytools.com/interlinear-bible/ passage.aspx?q=Matthew+25%3A12&t=kjv Retrieved: September 09, 2013.

CHAPTER 2

1 Edgar C. Whisenant, *88 Reasons Why The Rapture Will Be In 1988*, (USA: World Bible Society, 1988).

CHAPTER 3

1 John & Carol Arnott, *Grace & Forgiveness* (UK: New Wine Press, 2009, 2010).

2 Wikipedia, "Gratitude". Publish date unknown. Updated: August 21, 2013. http://en.wikipedia.org/ wiki/Gratitude#Association_with_well-being Retrieved: August 21, 2013.

CHAPTER 4

1 Marc Dupont, *Marc Dupont Ministries*, marcdupontministries.com Retrieved: September 07, 2013.

2 Stacy Campbell, *Revival Now! Ministries*, revivalnow.com Retrieved: August 02, 2013.

3 Larry Randolf, *Larry Randolf Ministries*, larryrandolph.com/about Retrieved: August 02, 2013.

4 Claudio Freidzon, claudiofreidzon.com Retrieved: August 02, 2013.

5 Randy Clark, *Global Awakening*, GlobalAwakening.com Retrieved: September 07, 2013.

6 Mark & Patti Virkler, *4 Keys to Hearing God's Voice*, (USA: Destiny Image 2010).

7 Search for "10 Minute Worship Revolution" on Facebook.

8 Revival Magazine article, Beni Johnson, "Winning Wars with 10 Minute worship". Published: March 09, 2012. http://revivalmag.com/article/winning-wars-10-minute-worship Retrieved: August 02, 2013.

CHAPTER 5

1 Charles Dickens, *A Tale Of Two Cities*, (UK: Chapman and Hall 1859).

2 World Health Organization, "Global Alert and Response (GAR) Severe acute respiratory syndrome (SARS)", copyright WHO 2013. Reports dated March 16, 2003 to May 18, 2004. http://www.who.int/csr/ don/archive/disease/severe_acute_respiratory_syndrome/en/index.html. Retrieved: August 02, 2013.

Public Health Reviews, Vol. 32, No 1, Antoine Flahault MD & Patrick Zylberman, "Influenza pandemics: past, present and future challenges" p.328. Press EHESP, France. Published: July 2010. http://www. publichealthreviews.eu/upload/pdf_files/7/18_Flahaut_final.pdf Retrieved: August 02, 2013.

3 Ibid. p.319.

4   Telegraph Media Group Limited article, "Arab Spring: timeline of the African and Middle East rebellions". Published: UK October 20, 2011. http://www.telegraph.co.uk/news/worldnews/africa andindianocean/libya/8839143/Arab-Spring-timeline-of-the-African-and-Middle-East-rebellions. html Retrieved: August 02, 2013.

5   NBC News article, Becky Bratu, "Connecticut school shooting is second worst in US history". Published: December 14, 2012. http://usnews.nbcnews.com/_news/2012/12/14/15909827-connecticut -school-shooting-is-second-worst-in-us-history?lite Retrieved: August 02, 2013.

6   NBC News article, Erin McClam, "Explosions rock finish of Boston Marathon; 3 killed and scores injured". Published: April 15, 2013. http://usnews.nbcnews.com/_news/2013/04/15/17764747-explosions -rock-finish-of-boston-marathon-3-killed-and-scores-injured?lite Retrieved: August 02, 2013.

7   US Geological Survey, "2013 Significant Earthquakes Archive". Published: July 08, 2013. http:// earthquake.usgs.gov/earthquakes/eqinthenews/2004/us2004slav/#summary Retrieved: Aug 02, 2013.

8   Earthquake-report.com article, "Japan Tohoku tsunami and earthquake: The death toll is climbing again!" Published: August 15, 2011. http://earthquake-report.com/2011/08/04/japan-tsunami-following- up-the-aftermath-part-16-june/ Retrieved: August 02, 2013.

9   Guardian News and Media Limited article, Greg Neale, "How an Icelandic volcano helped spark the French Revolution". Published: UK April 15, 2010. http://www.theguardian.com/world/2010/ apr/15/iceland-volcano-weather-french-revolution Retrieved: August 02, 2013.

10   Telegraph Media Group Limited article, "BP Leak the World's Worst Accidental Oil Spill". Published: UK August 03, 2010. http://www.telegraph.co.uk/finance/newsbysector/energy/oilandgas/7924009/ BP-leak-the-worlds-worst-accidental-oil-spill.html Retrieved: August 02, 2013.

11   The New York Times Company article, Aubrey Belford & Kevin Drew, "Australia Rushes Aid to Flooded Areas as Toll Rises". Published: January 03, 2011. http://www.nytimes.com/2011/01/04/ world/asia/04australia.html. Retrieved: August 02, 2013.

12   Blacksaturdaybushfires.com, "Black Saturday Bushfires". Copyright © 2013 Black Saturday Bushfires. http://www.blacksaturdaybushfires.com.au/ Retrieved: August 23, 2013.

13   Guardian News and Media Limited article, "Britain's big freeze continues". Published: UK December 02, 2010. http://www.theguardian.com/uk/gallery/2010/dec/02/britain-big-freeze -continues#/?picture=369303943&index=0 Retrieved: August 02, 2013.

14   Earthquake-report.com article, "Christchurch – 1 year after the devastating quake". Published: February 24, 2012. http://earthquake-report.com/2012/02/21/christchurch-1-year-after-the-dev- astating-quake/ Retrieved: August 02, 2013.

15   Homefacts.com, "Goodrich Township Tornado Information". Copyright © 2013 Homefacts.com http://www.homefacts.com/tornadoes/Michigan/Genesee-County/Goodrich.html Retrieved: August 13, 2013.

16   The Chronicle of Higher Education, Derek Quizon, "In Tornado's Aftermath, Difficult Decisions for 2 North Carolina Colleges". Published: April 19, 2011. http://chronicle.com/article/In-Tornados -Aftermath/127205/ Retrieved: August 13, 2013.

17   US Department of Commerce, National Oceanic and Atmospheric Administration Service Assessment, "The Historic Tornadoes of April 2011", p. iv. Published: December 2011. http://www. nws.noaa.gov/os/assessments/pdfs/historic_tornadoes.pdf Retrieved: August 13, 2013.

18   CBC News article, "Fire Destroys 40% of Slave Lake". Published: May 16, 2011. http://www.cbc.ca/news/canada/edmonton/story/2011/05/16/slave-lake-fire-evacuation.html Retrieved: August 13, 2013.

19   Cable News Network article, "Hurricane Sandy Fast Facts". Published: July 13, 2013. http://www.cnn.com/2013/07/13/world/americas/hurricane-sandy-fast-facts Retrieved: August 21, 2013.

     LiveScience, Tim Sharp, "Superstorm Sandy: Facts About the Frankenstorm". Published: November 27, 2012. http://www.livescience.com/24380-hurricane-sandy-status-data.html Retrieved: August 13, 2013.

20   CBC News article, "Toronto's July storm cost insurers $850M". Published: August 14, 2013. http://www.cbc.ca/news/business/story/2013/08/14/business-insurance-flooding.html Retrieved: August 21, 2013.

     The Huffington Post, Huffpost Alberta article, "Alberta Flood Costs Well Over $5 Billion: Redford". Published: August 19, 2013. http://www.huffingtonpost.ca/2013/08/19/alberta-flood-cost-over-5-billion_n_3781513.html Retrieved: August 21, 2013.

21   European Geosciences Union 2013, Geophysical Research Abstracts, "Three-dimensional simulation of extreme runup heights during the 2004 Indonesian and 2011 Japanese tsunamis". © Author(s) 2012 http://meetingorganizer.copernicus.org/EGU2013/EGU2013-1760.pdf Retrieved: August 13, 2013.

22   24-7 Prayer International article, Alana Wiens, "1 Million Haitians Pray: 3000 Saved". Published: March 03, 2010. http://www.24-7prayer.com/blog/1190 Retrieved: August 19, 2013.

CHAPTER 6

1   Korea.net, Global Communication and Contents Division, "Religion", Copyright © 1999–2013 KOCIS. Source: Statistics Korea www.kostat.go.kr http://www.korea.net/AboutKorea/Korean-Life/Religion Retrieved: August 14, 2013.

2   The Economist Newspaper Limited article, "O come all ye faithful". Published: November 1, 2007. http://www.economist.com/node/10015239 Retrieved: August 22, 2013.

3   International Movie Database, *1040: Christianity in the New Asia* (USA: Arowana Films, Asian Digital Ventures Network, 2010). http://www.imdb.com/title/tt1609920/ Retrieved: August 20, 2013.

4   Harvest International Ministry, "Pastor Che's Letter". Published: April 2013. http://harvestim.org/_news/april_2013/index.php Retrieved: August 20, 2013.

5   La Red Business Network, "Government and Institutional Training". Copyright © 2013 La Red Business Network. http://www.lared.org/government/ Retrieved: August 15, 2013.

6   Joel C. Rosenberg, *Inside the Revolution: How the Followers of Jihad, Jefferson, and Jesus are Battling to Dominate the Middle East and Transform the World,* (USA: Tyndale 2009, 2011) pp. 387–388.

CHAPTER 7

1   The Temple Institute, "About the Temple Institute". Copyright ©1991–2013, The Temple Institute. http://www.templeinstitute.org/about.htm Retrieved: August 22, 2013.

2   Israel National News, Hillel Fendel, "Temple Institute Announces: High Priest's Crown is Ready!" Published: February 12, 2007. http://www.israelnationalnews.com/News/News.aspx/124443#.UhZZmq6vd1N Retrieved: August 22, 2013.

3   NASA, "Five Millennium Catalog of Lunar Eclipses 1901 to 2000 (1901 CE to 2000 CE)". Published: May 23, 2011. http://eclipse.gsfc.nasa.gov/LEcat5/LE1901-2000.html Retrieved: August 16, 2013.

4   NASA, "Total Lunar Eclipse". Published: October 19th, 2004. http://www.nasa.gov/vision/universe/watchtheskies/13oct_lunareclipse.html Retrieved:August 15th, 2013.

5   NASA, "Lunar Eclipse Page". Published: July 08, 2013. http://eclipse.gsfc.nasa.gov/lunar.html Retrieved: August 16, 2013.

    Hebcal Jewish Calendar, "Jewish Holidays 2013-2014". Published: August 12, 2013. http://www.hebcal.com/holidays/2013-2014 Retrieved: August 16, 2013.

    Hebcal Jewish Calendar, "Jewish Holidays 2014-2015". Published: 12 August, 2013. http://www.hebcal.com/holidays/2014-2015 Retrieved: August 16, 2013.

    Hebcal Jewish Calendar, "Sukkot / תוכוס". Published: August 12, 2013. http://www.hebcal.com/holidays/sukkot Retrieved: August 16, 2013.

6   Hebcal Jewish Calendar, "Jewish Calendar 1949". Published: August 13, 2013. http://www.hebcal.com/hebcal/?year=1949&v=1&month=x&yt=G&nh=on&nx=on&i=off&vis=on&set=on&c=off&geo=zip Retrieved: August 16, 2013.

    Hebcal Jewish Calendar, "Jewish Calendar 1950". Published: August 13, 2013. http://www.hebcal.com/hebcal/?year=1950&v=1&month=x&yt=G&nh=on&nx=on&i=off&vis=on&set=on&c=off&geo=zip Retrieved: August 16, 2013.

    NASA, "Five Millennium Catalog of Lunar Eclipses 1901 to 2000 (1901 CE to 2000 CE)". Published: May 23, 2011. http://eclipse.gsfc.nasa.gov/LEcat5/LE1901-2000.html Retrieved: August 16, 2013.

7   US Department of State, Office of the Historian, "Milestones: 1945-1952". Publish date unknown. http://history.state.gov/milestones/1945-1952/CreationIsrael Retrieved: August 20, 2013.

8   Hebcal Jewish Calendar, "Jewish Calendar 1967". Published: August 13, 2013. http://www.hebcal.com/hebcal/?year=1967&v=1&month=x&yt=G&nh=on&nx=on&vis=on&set=on&c=off&zip= Retrieved: August 20, 2013.

    Hebcal Jewish Calendar, "Jewish Calendar 1968". Published: August 13, 2013. http://www.hebcal.com/hebcal/?year=1968&v=1&month=x&yt=G&nh=on&nx=on&vis=on&set=on&c=off Retrieved: August 20, 2013.

    NASA, "Five Millennium Catalog of Lunar Eclipses". Published: May 23, 2011. http://eclipse.gsfc.nasa.gov/LEcat5/LE1901-2000.html Retrieved: August 16th, 2013.

9   Israel Ministry of Foreign Affairs, "The Six Day War (June 1967)". Copyright all rights reserved to the State of Israel © 2013. http://mfa.gov.il/MFA/AboutIsrael/History/Pages/The%20Six-Day%20War%20-%20June%201967.aspx Retrieved: August 23, 2013.

10 New York Times Company article, Nazila Fathi, "Wipe Israel 'off the map' Iranian says". Published: October 27, 2005. http://www.nytimes.com/2005/10/26/world/africa/26iht-iran.html?_r=0 Retrieved: August 22, 2013.

11 NASA Goddard Space Flight Center, "Total Solar Eclipse of 2015 Mar 20". Published: February 07, 2008. http://eclipse.gsfc.nasa.gov/SEplot/SEplot2001/SE2015Mar20T.GIF Retrieved: August 23, 2013.

    Hebcal, "Jewish Holidays 2014-2015". Published: August 21, 2013. http://www.hebcal.com/holidays/2014-2015 Retrieved: August 23, 2013.

    NASA "Five Millennium Catalog of Lunar Eclipses 2001 to 2100 (2001 CE to 2100 CE)". Published: May 23, 2011. http://eclipse.gsfc.nasa.gov/LEcat5/LE2001-2100.html Retrieved: August 23, 2013.

About the Authors

John and Carol Arnott are the Founding Pastors of Catch The Fire Toronto (formerly known as the Toronto Airport Christian Fellowship) and are Presidents of Catch The Fire World. They are also overseers of the Partners in Harvest network of churches around the world. As international speakers, John and Carol have become known for their ministry of revival in the context of the Father's saving and restoring love. As the Holy Spirit moves with signs and wonders, they have seen millions of lives touched and changed through God's power and Christ's love.

John attended Ontario Bible College (now Tyndale College) in the late 1960's and then pursued a successful career in business. In 1980, while on a ministry trip to Indonesia, John and Carol responded to God's call on their lives for full-time ministry. Upon returning home, they started Jubilee Christian Fellowship in Stratford, Ontario in 1981. The Lord then called them to Toronto in 1987, where Toronto Airport Christian Fellowship was started. In January 1994, through a sovereign outpouring of the Holy Spirit, revival exploded into protracted nightly meetings which continued for 12 years, as the church came to the world's attention as a place where God was meeting with His people.

John is known for his teachings on the Father's love, grace and forgiveness and the Holy Spirit's power. He continues to impart wise counsel and provides a strong framework for those who want to see the power of God manifest in their church. Carol is especially known for her teachings on intimacy and soaking.

John and Carol live in the Greater Toronto Area. They have four adult children and five grandchildren. They travel extensively while continuing to oversee Catch The Fire and Partners in Harvest networks of churches.

Catch The Fire Toronto is a city-wide church in Toronto with multiple campuses and thousands of vibrant members from many diverse and ethnic backgrounds.

Catch The Fire World is our international church planting and outreach arm for conferences, schools and churches. Partners in Harvest (PIH) & Friends in Harvest (FIH) is our church network of over 500 churches internationally in over 50 nations.